PIMPGAME
204
T.H.E
P.I.M.
PIMPGAME
WISDOM
TJCLEMONS

Pimp Game 204

"The IZM"

Pimp

Game

Wisdom

TJ Clemons

itbftr@yahoo.com

Introduction

The "IZM" is the study, science, and mathematics of pimping.

It basically governs the pimp philosophy and the pimp commandments.

The Pimping is in you, not on you. You can't wear it like a t shirt.

When you let a bitch come through the door, make sure she has your

money first. Because if you're going to take a chance with her, then you

need some cash in advance. If she wants you to be her friend, then the

bitch needs to come with some dividends. Don't chase behind a hoe.

Tell her ass that you don't need her. She needs you. Why would you

even chase a bitch? Because the one that is being chased is in control.

Don't chase the bitch, replace the bitch. You can't be my friend and be

my bitch too. I don't need you to be my friend or to drive my Bendz.

You can back up off me like hot coffee. Move around bitch.

Back the fuck up before you get smacked the fuck up bitch.

Tell her your goals and expectations before you send her outside.

Her mission is to get you your money. Give her the game plan.

Because if you fail to plan, then you plan to fail, and you're not

focused on what is right in front of your face.

Plan your work and work your plan. I love that bankroll she gives me.

Never be an unbeliever or an underachiever. Don't down me.

Crown me. And don't bring any mother fucking bullshit around me.

The 10 Pimp Commandments Are:

1. Purse First Ass Last (Make Sure They Get Their Money Up Front)
2. Don't Chase Them Replace Them
3. When Pimping Begins Your Friendship Ends
4. You Must Plan Your Work And Work Your Plan
5. Give A Bitch Some Inspiration And Motivation Daily
6. Cop And Blow (Make Sure That They're Down For You)
7. A Hoe Without Instructions Is Headed For Her Self-Destruction
8. Grind For Your Shine
9. The Bigger The Instruction The More Production She Gives You
10. The Game Is To Be Sold Not Told

It's a cold mother fucking game but once you learn how to move

accordingly to its rules and regulations then you're going to advance by

leaps and bounds over time.

And make sure your girls know how to get their money before they give

up any of that sweet honey. Don't ever trust a trick.

Once she gives it up to a square mother fucker without getting paid in

advance that mother fucker has no incentive to break bread with a

bitch. He is going to try to lay her and play her instead of pay her.

It's human nature to try to get over on a weaker opponent.

So, she has to follow the rules correctly to avoid any bullshit and drama

with a mother fucker that is looking for a chance to get over on the

weaker opponent.

It's a mother fucking chess game and the king and queen play to win

and outsmart their opponents. The other mother fuckers are always

looking for signs of weakness to exploit.

Don't let a mother fucking trick play you like a pawn.

Use your status as my queen to keep his ass in check at all times.

I gave you all of this mother fucking good game for a reason.

You represent me everywhere that you go and with every move that

you make on this chess board called the streets. So, don't disappoint

me or there will be consequences and repercussions for your actions.

I put this game plan together. Now execute it like my queen and

partner in crime. The universe and the world belong to us forever

because we are married to this game together until death do us part.

Welcome to The "IZM"
Pimp Game Wisdom. Shut the fuck up!
And Pay Full Mother Fucking Attention

I grew up admiring and looking up to pimps, players, and Macks.

The difference between a pimp and a Mack is that a pimp starts up

from the bottom and works his way up in the game.

You start off as a player and then grow into becoming a pimp when you

start having enough game to motivate girls to want to handle your

business by choosing to selling their bodies for you.

A Mack is a pimp who really has his game together.

He is pimping at the highest level in the game.

His is often referred to as a Mack Daddy or a Mack.

That's exactly why they named the famous pimp movie The Mack.

The main character had elevated his game to the Mack level.

I started off in this game at the tender age of 17.

 I had met an older lady that was into prostitution that influenced

me into becoming her pimp.

She was even bold enough to ask my mother to let me pimp her.

My mother told her no, but I had already made my own mind up,

and I wanted to jump into this game feet first without a parachute on.

I was messing around with her for a few years and she used to give me

money all the time.

As a teenager I really didn't know anything about the game.

I just knew that she was a prostitute and I liked it when she gave me

all her money. It gave me an amazing feeling that is hard to describe.

She liked me all of those years and she wanted me to pimp her.

That's exactly how I got introduced to the game and got my feet wet.

Then I graduated and moved on to something bigger with her.

It became the trendy thing to do back then because we all grew up in

poverty and we were all looking for a way out and to make money.

And when the chance came up I took it, because I had a beautiful

woman who was willing to pay me money to be with her.

When I got into the life I had players that were 20 years older than me

that started giving me the game because they liked the way that I

carried myself out in the streets. And they took me under their wing

and they started feeding me the game on a professional level.

All the older players, pimps, and Macks wanted me to be better than

what they were at handling my business correctly in the game.

Out of all the youngsters coming up at that time they wanted me to be

the best and most gamed up individual. I don't know what they were

looking at or what they saw in me. I had very little life experience.

And I still follow the steps that were given by them to me years ago.

You have to have personal style. You have to have your tools in order.

You have to spread your wings like Bat Man. If you don't know much,

then you can't do much because the game is played smooth.

If you don't have knowledge of this game and how it goes then you

definitely won't be successful at it. It was passed down by the older

gentlemen down to the young players who had more experience.

The older guys would give them the same information that we are still

standing on today. And if they noticed that you weren't respecting the

game then they would pull you out of it and kick you to the left side

and tell them that they weren't ready to get with the game.

And now all the young guys look up to me as a gentleman of leisure.

I always handle my business and I never run out of game because if

you start running out of game then you're going to start running out of

money because these females are going to start running out of interest,

and you're pretty much played out to them. And they are going to

move on to someone more interesting with a lot more game than you.

I still continue to elevate my game and take it to another level.

All I do is dress, and rest, and ride. And that's all that I have ever done.

They are always trying to say that I'm doing this and I'm doing that.

I'm not guilty of none of it because all I do is mind my business and

mind my money. And there is nothing criminal about that.

I just cover all of my bases and keep winning.

I still run the same program that I have for all of these years.

Knowledge is power because if you don't know much then you can't

do much of anything. You have to know something for women to

respect you. And everybody is going to respect you when they see

you on top of your game.

I went to prison and didn't lose anything. I got a house built from the

ground up while I was in there. It all about knowledge and what you

know about what's going on in the world around you.

I accept money from my women from time to time.

But you have to know what you're doing and how to spend it wisely.

Money will soon depart from a foolish mother fucker quickly.

I been down with this game for years and I have records that will

never be broken and they still stand today against the hands of time.

And all the guys who gave the game to me were proud of my

achievements. They were my mentors in the game and they all wanted

me to be better than them and they wanted me to stand up and

stand out everywhere because I represented the game given to me.

I didn't want to take their position because I respected them so much.

And I pass my game on to the next generation when I can, because I

stand up top and I stay up top in the game.

I'm still on top because I handle my business because of the knowledge

and game that I was taught as a young player.

I learned a little bit of something from everybody coming up.

All of them weren't winners but some of the things that I learned

from them were valuable and they made me who I am today.

I learned to look for women who were dedicated to their man.

They have to be qualified enough to listen to my instructions and my

my guidance that I am giving them. And I want them be down for me

100 percent. So, they have to be down by law.

These women today are really head strong and most of them don't

want to listen to the average man. You really have to pimp them.

They will try to tell you something if you're not sharp enough to

 tell them the ins and outs of the game.

So, you really have to be about your business with them.

You can't layoff with them because then it's not going to pay off.

You have to get down and dirty with them and handle your business.

They really have to be able to respect you as their man.

When they get out of line you have to check them right then and there.

You don't never stop being a man and that's what they are going to

honor and respect about you and your game.

I was on top of the world and I did a friend a favor that was in the dope

game and they stripped me and took everything from me on that

particular case. It cost me everything doing him a favor.

The only thing I was really guilty of at the time was dressing, resting,

and riding around in luxury automobiles. Sometimes doing favors for

close friends can cost you.

You have to be careful when you move different outside of your

comfort zone and the game is going to charge for making those kinds

of costly mistakes. That time it caught me a drug case.

I don't deal drugs only women but that's what they charged me with

because I was moving too fast and friendly in that moment.

That was the perception put on me from law enforcement officers

because they were jealous of my lifestyle and they couldn't figure out

how to get to the next level and live like a king like I was doing.

They didn't understand the mindset that you could have a bigger

playing field to play on like us players in the pimping game.

Instead of them leveling up like us mentally, they wanted to destroy

everything that we worked hard for because that gives them their

joy and satisfaction in life. That's a very sick mentality if you ask me.

Even as a pimp you're only going to be big as the ones who taught you

the game. And I learned mine from giants.

I stuck by the script they gave me because it worked and I added on to

it when I figured out something new and interesting.

I was smart in school and used that same knowledge in the streets.

My women can only get so much money for pussy for so long.

Then they learn how to use their wits to scam tricks out of their money.

Some of these tricks want to get robbed because they try to impress

these women with large amounts of money. That's definitely a mistake.

If a mother fucker puts himself in that position then it's going to

happen one way or another because once she sees all that money

she is going to find a way to get it and give it to her pimp.

Just like I said before, a fool and his money will soon depart.

It's part of the game. They use to bring me so much money that I had to

start questioning them about it. I had to know where it came from

because I'm basically part of the conspiracy if I was there or not, when

they took it from a mother fucker.

They learn how to steal from other prostitutes.

They don't think that I know it, but as long as the money keeps coming

in then I'm down with it. They have to be good at it though because

money obviously brings drama and a whole lot of bull shit with it.

This game is orchestrated by choice and not by force.

We don't make women prostitute themselves against their will.

That is looked down upon in our circle. We don't do that.

All we do is talk to them about it because women are naturally going

to be promiscuous. And all they need is the right man with guidance.

Because a man thinks from his mind and women are guided by their

emotions and feelings. She might know how to go out there and use

her talents to get money, but she needs a man to know what to do with

it, so they are both successful in the long run.

If the man isn't good with their money and messes it up all the time,

then that women who is working hard to get paid is going to find

another man who knows how to manage it better.

I always stuck by the rules of the game and played fair with my women.

These females are not going to stick around if you bullshit and play

games with them and their money. And I stand on it.

I changed the game by elevating my whole life and my experiences.

The average mother fucker couldn't comprehend or understand the

way that I think and feel. I'm so far ahead of their limited mindsets.

I'm light years ahead of them.

I don't get mad or upset because they don't really understand where

I'm coming from. But some of them choose to hate on men like me.

They don't understand how I'm doing what I'm doing in the game.

I doing everything on an above average level.

And they sit around looking amazed and dumb founded.

I'm at the top of the food chain and they are still guppies.

I know guys who wanted to be pimps and they had girls working for

them and they were never even able buy themselves a car.

Him and his girls walked everywhere that they went. And they could

never advance in the game enough to even by themselves a vehicle.

I have been buying brand new cars for years myself.

Your dress code, houses, and your cars show your lifestyle.

And you have to be living a certain type of way to be a real pimp.

You just can't talk the game. You have to walk the game as well.

A lot of these pimps are just blowing wind.

They scream it but they don't really mean it.

I'm serious about what I do and what it takes to be a pimp.

I started off driving brand new Cadillac's for years.

Then square mother fuckers started driving Cadillac's, and you couldn't

even tell the difference between the real pimps and players so I had to

jump up into more luxurious vehicles.

I always wanted to be on top and drive something that the average

mother fucker couldn't afford. I started buying their dream cars.

That in itself shows you the level of your game.

That's what real players and pimps do when they reach that level.

That's what the game is all about.

I started off a regular kid from childhood going to school.

I went to church on Sunday's and I came from a good family.

They raised me up to become an upstanding citizen.

I worked hard at everything no matter what it was.

Most people who I grew up around were uneducated and unskilled.

They didn't have much going for themselves other than survival skills.

I started off trying to work square jobs but they never worked out.

I ended up getting interested in street hustles to get my income from.

We were all struggling but I knew that there had to be a better way.

The women really liked me so I started hustling them more and more.

I did what I could do best to try and do street hustles to survive.

I started my street education with the players and pimps every day.

I wanted to live the fast life like they were doing.

I started getting seasoned in the game. They sprinkled me daily with it.

I started to become wiser because the game was choosing me.

It kind of fell into my lap because I was in the right place at the right

time to learn from these seasoned veterans in the pimping game.

I never thought that I would become internationally known.

I'm one of the greatest that ever played this here game.

I'm one of the most successful pimps that ever lived.

I had the best cars, clothes, and the best women.

I came up under real players and pimping mother fuckers.

I was very fortunate to be in that position and I still am.

The type of people that you're around and influence you is a very

good reflection of what you're going to become in this game.

A shark can only grow 8 feet in a fish tank but 80 feet in the ocean.

You are going to pimp at the level of the pimps around you.

So, you have to move around and think outside of the box.

Pimping is all about growth and opportunities.

The situation that I was in put me in a place to be ahead of the game.

Even though I was in the streets I always put god first and foremost.

I don't take less. And I only accept the best of everything.

I don't want to be a survivor because my ambition is to thrive.

I became what I was taught to be and I keep that same mentality.

You have to do well and work hard for everything that you want.

I don't compromise. I go after everything that my heart desires.

I have been that same way since my childhood days.

You have to keep that mentality and have a strong will to succeed.

A lot of people give up on everything the first chance that they get.

And they fall by the waste side and sink like the Titanic.

I have a totally different attitude and concept about myself.

You are broke from your mindset. Most people have a broke mentality.

They become victims of their own surroundings.

They listen to skepticism and doubt all the time.

They need to surround themselves with successful individuals.

I used to ride by rich people's houses when I was a child and wonder

why we weren't living the lifestyles that they were living.

I couldn't figure out why we were living in poverty, while they were

living in prosperity. It didn't make any sense in my young mind.

I knew that something just wasn't right about it.

But eventually I got on their level and moved to the suburbs.

It wasn't overnight. I really had to put some work in to get there.

I never wanted to live around poverty and crime once I figured it out.

I always wanted something bigger and better.

And I still have that same mentality and drive today.

I wanted my children to go to good schools and live in prosperity.

I was focused on taking care of them and giving them a good life.

I wanted my parents to drive luxury cars and live in a bigger house.

And I am pretty sure that my kids are going to want that for the

next generation that they are going to bring into existence.

My children were my first priority.

I have one son who grew up and got into the game.

He is a shining reflection of his father and I'm very proud of him.

I want him to take the pimping game to the next level.

He is the perfect image of me and I give him game all of the time.

He has his own mindset and I respect it.

I try not to tell him what to do but I do tell him what not to do.

I help him as much as I can with his journey into the game.

I was always destined for greatness in the game.

I was born with the right mentality for it. It was a perfect fit for me.

I still believe in myself and I still try to get better at pimping.

As time goes on it moves forward. You can't get stuck in the past.

You have to always elevate your thinking and your thought process.

Most people don't think for themselves because they are trained to

follow the latest trend or they try to copy what everybody else is doing.

They don't have a single original thought for themselves.

There are a lot more sheep than shepherds in our society today.

I don't fall in that category at all because I was born a leader.

There is an obvious generational gap in the game.

We worked a lot harder to get ahead and stay ahead by miles.

We just thought about things differently.

Some of these new guys were raised by teenage mothers and fathers.

So, they just are going to be born and bred into wisdom and knowledge

the same way that we were. They were mostly born followers.

They follow every new trend and concept like it's the gospel.

They want to become rappers, gang bangers, and pimps because

that's what their friends and family members are doing.

The next generation might be totally different and become leaders.

A lot of people in this generation just aren't doing anything.

But they want to criticize people who are working hard to get paid.

There are a lot of broke pimps, players, and hustlers today.

The guys selling dope are walking and the dope fiends are driving.

The dope dealers are homeless and they are living with their clients.

It's totally opposite of the way that I came up.

We were poor but we worked hard to get ahead.

The drug game is ruling everything all over the world.

Most people wanted money when I was coming up.

Now they just want to get high and listen to their music.

The drug dealers are on more drugs than their customers sometimes.

And snitching has fucked up the dope game all together.

You can't even make enough money to take a chance on incarceration.

They have become slaves to drugs instead of money.

You used to be able get rich off of the dope game quickly.

Now you might have a six month run and get locked up from snitches.

There is no loyalty and respect like it was back then.

It's not even worth taking a chance selling drugs anymore.

Your freedom is very short lived in the dope game.

People are beginning to start more legit businesses and enterprises.

Only a small percentage really have that mindset and mentality though.

We need more advancement into thinking and growing into prosperity.

It really needs to be adapted more into our culture and society.

We need fast independent thinkers and innovators.

We are all born with different gifts and talents but a lot of people

are scared to tap into their natural resources because they don't want

to be looked at differently from the status quo individuals that they

are surrounded by.

They think pimping is easy because I make I look that way.

It's not easy at all. It's a constant battle against a lot of negative forces.

And you have to be smart enough to adjust to different circumstances

and situations at a moment's notice.

And you also have to know how to put your pride to the side when it's

time to get down and keep these females motivated to get your money.

They have been misled and misguided into believing that the pimping

game is going to always be quick, simple, and non-problematic.

It just doesn't work that way. You constantly have to make adjustments

and in the moment decisions that are going to affect your ability to

keep money flowing into your direction and into your pockets.

You have to be able to adjust to a lot of moving parts that are all

going in different directions all day and night long.

It takes a certain type of mother fucker to be able to handle all of it.

You really have to know how to handle our women and keep them

in line when they get out of pocket. You have to be in control of her

mind in order to control what she needs to do with her body.

It can be a complicated process sometimes.

You have to be able to reinvent yourself daily and come up with new

game for your women so that they don't lose interest in what you're

telling them and instructing them to do.

You have to be aware of the competition from other pimps and

their prostitution partners. You have to know how to utilize your

women to gain information on what is going on in the prostitution

game on a daily basis. They will become your eyes and ears in all kinds

of different circumstances and situations that are going to come to you.

You have to adapt daily. The street life and culture is rapidly changing.

A lot of things now are going down through the internet because they

are really starting to go after pimps to give them trafficking charges.

It's really a money game. The government doesn't really care about

pimps or prostitutes. They care about keeping up the image of being

hard on crime and hard on criminals and compassionate to prey.

Prostitutes are now being looked at as victims of human trafficking.

And pimps are often being labeled as human traffickers.

It's the current agenda and policy that is going on in law enforcement.

It's just another way for the government to make money off of

pimps who are primarily African American men.

And they are funneling government funds into women's shelters

and different types of government agencies who make large profits.

It all comes down to the almighty dollar.

They want money for locking up pimps and they also make money

"helping" human trafficking victims. It's a vicious cycle of drama,

bullshit, and making money off of all kinds of human misery.

They in fact are making huge profits off of trafficking human beings.

It's just a more complicated version of the three card Monte.

They are the hustlers who are getting paid off of it.

They have just repacked and reinvented themselves as the hero.

They cause the drama and uproot people and move them around

all in the name of law and order when they are really creating chaos

in the lives of a lot of men and women who are basically minding their

own fucking business and trying to make money to thrive and survive.

They are the inside mother fuckers in that game of controlling the lives

and futures of adults who are in most cases doing what they want to do

happily and freely of their own free will.

Then they lock these women up and give them a get out of jail free card

which includes housing and other government programs in exchange

for telling on the person who was out here helping them hustle and

survive on a daily basis. While you have been taking care of everything

for her day in and day out for years and years and sometimes decades.

They take away everything that she knows and loves in exchange for

free housing and food stamps while the man that she loves is

transported to a correctional facility to be "housed" for up to 30 to 60

years of his natural life. That's pretty much how the system is set up.

I have mastered this game over the years and I have learned to stay far

away from anything that my women are doing for me and them as well.

And you have to know how to choose your women wisely.

They have to qualify for that position of loyalty, faithfulness, love,

honesty, honor, and respect because she has to remain solid to you

and with you just like your wife in your marriage to the game.

Game recognizes game. Can't no random mother fucker just walk in

here and tell me anything and I fall for it like a sucker.

I can tell what that mother fucker is made of by the words the words

that are coming out of their mouths' and their eye contact, and by

their body language. The average mother fucker is full of shit anyways

and they are busy trying to blow smoke up your ass.

I can see them walking down the street and read their whole vibe and

personality. This is my career and my profession and I know exactly

how to deal with them on multiple levels.

You have to be educated in all aspects of the game.

You can't be out here second guessing or unsure of yourself.

That's a sign of weakness in this game and a mother fucker will try

his or her best to get over on you if you let them do it to you.

I have been swimming with sharks for a long mother fucking time.

And I refuse to be the meal in that situation.

I would rather be the predator than the prey any mother fucking day.

You have to be blessed into this game and you also have to know how

to use your blessings wisely every single mother fucking day.

You have to be in control of every possible scenario and situation.

Everybody doesn't automatically have the same thoughts and theories.

That's where confusion comes into the situation every time.

Your job is to lead mother fuckers, not to follow mother fuckers.

You have to elevate in this game and always be moving forward.

You have to stack your money and invest wisely.

The next mother fucker might fuck their money up every day and

expect his female partner to go out there the next day to do the exact

same thing and not have any money to fall back onto later on.

What happens if your woman runs off with another pimp?

She might get knocked and you need money to bail her out.

Females have a lot of physical problems naturally. So, when they are

selling their bodies they might run into even more issues with sexually

transmitted diseases, infections, or any other kind of ailment.

You have to be prepared for just about any circumstance or situation.

You can't just sit there stuck on stupid because you're the brains

behind the whole operation just like 'The Wizard of Oz'.

You have to know how to stack your money for bad times when the

money isn't coming in for whatever the reason may be.

A fool and his money depart quickly, just like I said before.

I have been the biggest fool in the world and I learned from it.

Mistakes are blessings in disguise because you learn valuable lessons.

I have lost more money than some people will make in their lifetime.

I have made foolish mistakes but I'm wise enough to admit them.

I preach to the youngsters so that they can learn from my mistakes.

They can avoid some of the pitfalls and traps that are set up for pimps.

Experience is the best teacher but some of us still don't listen.

But if you bump your head enough times you're going to buy yourself a

hard hat and learn how to move around more smoothly than before.

This game is full of traps that are designed for your destruction.

But sooner or later you are going to learn survival skills, because only

the strong mother fuckers survive and thrive in this game.

I don't worry about my future in this game, because I take life head on

and try to control as many situations as I can with me and my women.

If I don't know how to handle certain situations, then I make moves like

in a chess game and retreat so that I can stay alive long enough to fight

another battle in the overall war that is going on in the game eternally.

I'm a one man army. A lot of guys need to be surrounded by their

homeboys for protection like these gang bangers who set trip.

They need that security around them in order to feel safe from danger.

I take life situations head on by myself. So, however it comes to me,

that's exactly how I'm going to handle it when it comes my way.

I'm educated enough to take things to the next level and move

righteously against any one or anything that becomes a weapon formed

against me that was designed for my spiritual and physical destruction.

I believe in myself and I always have. And I know what it takes to win.

The worst time in my life is when I worked 20 straight years in the game

and I was pretty much secure for the rest of my natural life and I made

that one major mistake by trying to help a friend of mine and the

government took everything that I had and that I had worked hard for.

That was my worst life experience.

Anything can happen to you in life that you don't see coming.

We all think everything is all good and every situation is going to work

out the way that we want it to. But the unexpected can happen to any

of us without any warning and you can't prepare for every situation.

We think everything is going to be the same and flow in the same

direction forever, but the world changes every single day and we have

to learn how to adapt to those changes daily in order to survive.

We get so many blessings and lessons as part of the game structure.

I didn't have a single worry in the world at that time.

Then everything changed when I got caught up with my close friend.

I had eight women in my stable and I lost them all.

They all moved around and scattered in different directions.

They put me in a position where I had no other alternatives when I got

locked up and sent me very far away to a dark cold place called prison.

I couldn't handle my business or keep bringing in my money.

They had got a man who was a friend of my friend to make a mistake.

And when he got caught up he made the decision to take down

everybody around him and make a deal for himself for a reduced

prison sentence. And I ended up getting caught up in that storm.

Then it turned into a vicious circle of treachery and deceit.

My close friend who got set up used my name in vain and then he

helped the government put a case on me with some fake charges.

They ended up taking everything that I paid prostitution money for.

And the government claimed that I got it from selling drugs.

I never sold any drugs in my whole life. I only sold pussy.

That experience taught me a valuable lesson. You have to protect

yourself at all times from every single mother fucker that you come in

contact with on any level. I was so deep into the game and I thought

everybody that around me was solid but they collapsed under pressure.

At that time I wasn't protected from my own inner circle and people

who I called my friends. I was thinking that the people around me

would ever turn on me the way that they did. I trusted them.

And I felt safe around them. But I actually needed to be protected

from them and their ulterior motives.

They clearly disrespected the game that I believed in and leaned on as

my life line. But this was a very valuable lesson that I had to learn for

myself and for my future success in this game.

Going to prison on those trumped up charges was another valuable

lesson that I had to learn about health, education, what I didn't know

already about myself, what I needed to know about life, and how to

protect myself from the people closest to me.

I learned a lot when I went away for those 5 years.

When you're in the game you're surrounded by an umbrella of different

street hustles and hustlers. Some people sell drugs.

Some people do drugs. I was taught from a very young man about the

dope game. I knew the ins and outs of it. My hustle was women.

I never really indulged in using drugs.

I smoked a little bit of weed when I was in my early teen years.

And when I started pimping money was the only drug that I was ever

really addicted to because I was all about a dollar and trying to keep my

pockets full of dead presidents.

I learned how to get my money and then get out of the way.

That is exactly what the pimps, players, and Macks told me to do.

That took me out of any situation to even think about selling any drugs.

All I know how to do is dress, rest, and ride in luxury automobiles.

I like my lifestyle. I don't want to get caught up in any kind of drama.

I don't like to take any unnecessary chances with my freedom or my

life because I have been through that shit already.

And I learned from my past mistakes.

I'm retired from the game now and I own legit business establishments.

And don't think because you see me moving this way or that way that

you know what I'm all about. But what I do want you to know about me

is that I'm a mother fucking hustler and I'll be a hustler to the very

last day of my life on planet earth until I take my last breath.

I consider myself to be an entertainer because of my reputation.

People know me from the pimping game and they will never forget

how I put it down with all of my beautiful and exotic women.

I always liked looking good, dressing good, and smelling good.

There is absolutely nothing wrong with looking good and having money.

I'll never stop doing that because it's my job to represent the game.

And I always tell these youngsters to get educated and leave this street

life alone, because nothing good is going to come from it.

I even tell my own son the same thing but he is grown and has his own

mindset and ways of thinking. And I can only tell him what I know.

The rest is up to him. I'm very proud of him and he does actually listen

to me sometimes, which often leads him in the righteous direction.

He knows how to stay out of the way. And as long as he is alright,

then I'm alright and we are both living my best lives.

I take good care of everybody around me and treat them like family.

I'm a father to all my children and I'm in all of their lives.

I sometimes wish that my life took a different path and direction.

But at the end of the day it is what it is and you live and die by all of

the choices and decisions that you make daily and the hand you have.

When you come from where I came from you want to escape poverty.

You have to find a way out and pimping way my ladder to success.

The way it is now most working people are doing better than the

people involved in street hustles. So, I let these youngsters know that

you have to weigh your options wisely and do what is in your own

self-interest instead of following after another dumb mother fucker.

So, you have to think about it twice before you decide to jump into the

game full force because it its full of peril as well as prosperity.

People with jobs will probably never get as far as I did but most of them

are well off enough to do pretty good for themselves. And they have a

safe place to call home without looking over their shoulders all day.

By me growing up in that fish tank instead of the ocean I was

surrounded by the pimps, players, and hustlers and they showed me

the only way out that they knew of at the time to make me successful.

It wasn't a lot but at that time we were winning.

And I ended up becoming something spectacular in this game.

People still recognized me and I still feel like a local celebrity.

I wanted to live a regular normal life but the game chose me.

I chose the fast life even though the slow pace is known to win the race.

I wanted a proper education, but I ended up with a degree from the

streets and it made me into the man that I am today.

I have had a lot of interesting life experiences as well.

If I had known or actually been aware of all the options that I had a very

long time ago, then I probably would have taken another route in life.

Everything good isn't gold. You don't know everything that a person

has gone through in order to become a top notch player or pimp.

I had to run the streets with my girls and handle a whole lot of business

for them in order for my women to be successful at prostitution.

There is a lot of competition on all levels of the game.

People often glamorize this lifestyle because we make it look easy.

There is always more to it that it looks like from the outside looking

into it as a square individual. And that's why they don't respect the

game the same way that people who are involved with it do.

I have been blessed in this game because I had a lot more good days in

it, then I have had bad days in it. I have been enjoying those advantages

because I have been winning for a lot of years because I stayed on top

of my business every day and night as well.

You have to know how to play the game so that the game doesn't

play you. Always be a leader and not a follower.

You have to have your own mind, thoughts, and feelings and always

follow your first mind in situations and never second guess yourself.

There are a lot of haters around you who want to bring harm to you.

And they are preying every day for your downfall.

As a pimp you are always of in the presence of people with evil

motivations and intentions. It's just in their nature to be jealous and

envious of your success in the pimping game.

That type of energy follows you everywhere that you go.

It's just a natural part of the game. They don't want to be just like you.

They want to be you. And they will stab you in the back without a

moment's notice in order to try and take your place.

The most important lesson that I have learned is to be patient.

You also have to stay focused and keep yourself motivated to be

doing something positive and prosperous as much as you possibly can.

Get your education if you want to win in this world.

A lot of people waste their natural talents being stuck on stupid.

You have to be able to explore your options in order to be able to

tap into your full potential and know what you're truly capable of.

You might think that you're on the right path when something way

better is waiting for you in a totally different direction.

There was a guy who had oil on his land. He went across the country

searching for gold. He sold his house and moved out west.

Three years after he moved the next owners were digging up the

yard to start planting a garden and struck oil.

He moved away in search of gold and missed out on an oil well.

He didn't know it at the time but he was moving too fast.

Sometimes success is right there in front of you.

I think back to my younger days and I just didn't know better.

We are so busy moving around trying to make something happen

that we often missed out on smart investments and opportunities.

This is one of life's greatest lessons. If you don't know, then you can't

grow, I missed out on a few prospects when I was in the street life.

We learned how to be more knowledgeable when we miss out.

We didn't want to make those same mistakes over and over again.

You live and you learn, especially in the pimping game.

When I was coming up in the life a lot of guys that were dealing with

drugs were prostitutes too.

They were all moving around in the same circles. It was all in the game.

Pimping is not only exciting but you can eat pretty good off of it.

I fed a lot of people along the way and I gave a lot of women better

lifestyles and opportunities because they chose to be down with me.

And all of them did it by choice and not by force.

The broke mother fuckers hated me because they wanted to be me.

They get mad at me for working hard to get my money.

When all they really had to do was ask me to put them in the game,

and I could have showed them how to get their own girls and money.

That's some sucker shit. And I watch them mother fuckers like a

hawk everywhere that I go because they always wanted what I had.

This game is full of lessons and blessings and I'm very glad that the

game chose me. And I'm also glad that I chose the game.

This book is dedicated to the memory of my loving and beautiful auntie

Joyce Joann Watson who was born February 18th in the year of 1949,

she departed and left us missing her forever and dearly on the day of

March 2nd in the year of 2023.

Joyce Joann Watson was known as "Mama Joyce" everywhere,

especially in Youngstown Ohio , Atlanta Georgia, and all over the great

state of Florida. She touched my life and many more lives and she

always motivates her loved ones to be great.

She still inspires me daily because she was always proud of me.

Many wonderful things can be said about my aunt Joyce Watson, but

I'm going try and honorably to some her up at the moment simply with

two words from my own loving perspective of her.

She was and will always be a BEAUTIFUL QUEEN to me and everybody

was blessed to be able to know and love her deeply.

Joyce Watson expressed her love individually to all of us in her own

special and unique way. And she will be missed and loved by all of us

forever and eternally. And we will cherish all of our special memories

and moments with her. The world is forever changed without our

beloved queen Joyce Joann Watson